INTERFACT REFERENCE

SPACE

TWO CAN™

What's in the book?

What's on the disk?

You'll find a whole universe to explore! On opening the disk, you'll meet Captain Collins – your guide to space. Captain Collins will tell you how to use the disk and how to keep track of your progress in your own personal Data Station. Then, go exploring with your mouse! Each of the activities (see right) are hidden in a different part of the universe.

There are seven exciting activities for you to find!

Installing the Space CD-ROM

See page 48 for troubleshooting tips, system requirements and helpline details.

Windows 95 or 98
The Space program should start automatically when you put the CD into your CD-ROM drive. If it does not, follow these instructions.
1. Put the CD into the CD drive.
2. Double-click on My Computer.
3. Double-click on the CD drive icon.
4. Double-click on the SPACE icon.

Windows 3.1 or 3.11
1. Put the CD into the CD Drive.
2. Open File Manager.
3. Double-click on the CD drive icon.
4. Double-click on the SPACE icon.

Macintosh
1. Put the CD into the CD drive.
2. Double-click on the SPACE FOR MAC icon.

Power Macintosh
1. Put the CD into the CD drive.
2. Double-click on the SPACE FOR POWER MAC icon.

Cosmic Challenge

Meet the one and only Larry Lunar, the host of this challenging game show. Pick the character that you'd like to be, then take your chances against the opponent of your choice!

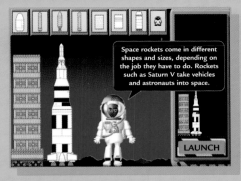

Liftoff

Here's your chance to build a rocket! All the pieces you'll need are on screen. When you've put the pieces in place, click on the launch button to see if your rocket gets off the ground.

Star Gazing

Fancy being an astronomer? Using the book to help you, put the pieces of the night sky into place. Then, use your mouse to explore the night sky and learn all about the stars and constellations.

Galactic Gallery

Visit the Galactic Gallery. You'll need to wake up Gerald, the friendly guard, from his afternoon nap. Then he'll help you to learn all about distant galaxies and play a fun memory game, too.

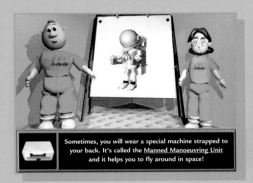

Space Cadet

Have you ever wondered what it would be like to be an astronaut? Well, here's your chance to find out! Have a go at this interactive adventure and see if you've got what it takes to travel into space!

Earth Alert

Emergency! A massive asteroid is plummeting towards Earth. If you're smart, you'll destroy the asteroid before it hits Earth! Just answer the quiz questions as they appear on screen.

Toolbar

The toolbar appears whenever you move the cursor to the right-hand edge of the screen.

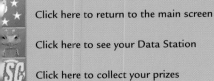

Click here to return to the main screen

Click here to see your Data Station

Click here to collect your prizes

Click here to use the glossary

Click here to use your notebook

Click here for help

Click here to quit

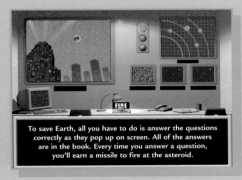

Solar System Mission

It's time to get to work. You are employed by Orbital, the biggest and best trucking company in the solar system. You'll get to travel to every planet in the solar system – but watch out for dangers along the way!

Glossary

Got a problem with a space word that's been used in the book or on the disk? Then look it up in the glossary! Use your toolbar to find this disk feature. It will certainly help you come to terms with all the space terminology!

What is space?

Space is the huge emptiness surrounding Earth. It stretches further than astronomers can see, even with their most powerful telescopes. In space, there are stars, **moons** and galaxies, and **planets,** including Earth. In between the planets and stars, there are tiny bits of dust and **gas.** Everything in space is part of the **universe.** There may be other things in the universe waiting to be discovered.

▶ Scientists think that the universe was formed about 10 to 20 **billion** years ago. These pictures show you what may have happened.

1 The universe probably began with a huge explosion that scientists call the Big Bang. Immediately after the Big Bang, the universe was small and very hot.

Big Bang

2 Then the universe cooled down and became larger. Huge swirls of dust and gas clung together to make galaxies.

galaxy

nebula

3 Inside the galaxies, there were smaller dust and gas clouds called nebulae. This is where the stars were born. One of these stars was the Sun. It was born in a galaxy called the Milky Way.

Earth

Mercury

Sun

Venus

solar system

Uranus

Mars

Jupiter

Saturn

Neptune

Pluto

4 Nine planets formed around the new Sun to make the solar system. One of these planets was Earth.

Go to Rocky planet page 30, Sun page 26

Earth

Earth is a huge ball of rock travelling through space. It is one of the nine **planets** that orbit the Sun. Earth is different from the other planets because much of its surface is covered with water. It is also the only planet known to have life. It is home to many kinds of plants and animals. These things can live here because Earth is just the right distance from the Sun, making it neither too hot nor too cold.

▼ This picture shows the different layers that make up Earth.

crust
The crust is the top, rocky layer of Earth. It forms all the land and the ocean floor.

mantle
Beneath the crust is a thick layer of hot rock called the mantle.

outer core
Hot, melted iron forms Earth's outer **core**.

.... daytime

Earth

Sun

night-time

Day and night
Earth spins round like a top. As it spins, only one side faces the Sun. The side facing the Sun has daytime and the side facing away has night-time.

Life on Earth

Three to four **billion** years ago, early forms of life appeared in the ocean. They were too small to see but they slowly developed into plants, jellyfish and fish.

About 360 million years ago, some fish began to change and spend part of their time on land. Later, they began to live on land all the time.

Around 240 million years ago, enormous dinosaurs roamed Earth. Suddenly, about 150 million years later, they were all wiped out.

Above Earth

The air round Earth keeps it warm and forms its **atmosphere**. Air is made up of several **gases**, including **oxygen**. Below, you can see the different layers of the atmosphere. As you move away from Earth, there is less air in the atmosphere until it disappears completely.

into space
Space begins where Earth's atmosphere ends.

80-450 km
A space shuttle flies at 200 km above Earth. There is hardly any air here.

50-80 km
Here, the air burns up tiny rocks from space to make meteors, or shooting stars.

ozone layer
Some of the Sun's rays can be harmful. A gas, called ozone, helps to stop these rays from reaching Earth.

11-50 km
Some jet planes fly in this layer of the atmosphere, above the clouds.

0-11 km
Close to Earth there is plenty of air. Most of the clouds are here.

inner core
At Earth's centre, the inner core is a hot ball of **solid iron**.

Factfile

It may reach 6,000°C at the centre of Earth. That's over 100 times hotter than the hottest desert.

Earth measures 40,075 km round its widest part. It would take one and a half years, travelling day and night, to walk all the way round.

Sometimes hot rock from inside Earth bursts out of the crust to form a **volcano***.*

About 200 million years ago, the first birds appeared on Earth. They had claws on their wings and probably developed from flying reptiles.

Humans have lived on Earth for about two million years. This is a short time compared with the dinosaurs. They lived on Earth about 80 times longer.

Go to Galaxy page 42, Telescope page 10

Astronomer

Astronomers are people who study objects in space, such as the Sun, Moon, stars and **planets**. They work out what these things are made of, where they are and how fast they are travelling. Many objects in space are so far away that astronomers need to use powerful telescopes to study them properly. Astronomers are always searching the skies for new discoveries and trying to see further into space than before.

Copernicus

Over 450 years ago, in 1543, a Polish astronomer called Copernicus suggested that all the planets, including Earth, travelled round the Sun. At the time, most other astronomers did not believe him. They could see the Sun move across the sky, so they believed that the Sun and the planets travelled round Earth. Today we know that these astronomers were wrong and that Copernicus' ideas were right.

The first astronomers

Long ago, the first astronomers used the movements of the Sun, Moon, stars and planets to help people plan their daily lives. Astronomers built towers, such as the one above, to watch the sky. By looking at the different positions of objects in the sky, they could tell when the seasons were about to change and work out the best time for farmers to plant their seeds. They could also tell the time by watching the Sun move across the sky during the day.

The wrong way

In Picture A, the Sun and the planets travel round Earth, so Earth is at the centre of the **universe**.

A

Earth

Sun

The right way

Picture B shows you how the planets really travel. Here the Sun is at the centre and Earth and the other planets travel round it.

B

Sun

Earth

Galileo

Over 350 years ago, in 1610, an Italian astronomer named Galileo discovered that the planet Jupiter had four **moons** circling round it. This proved that everything did not travel round Earth. It made people realise that Copernicus' ideas were right. In this picture you can see two of the telescopes Galileo used to make his discoveries.

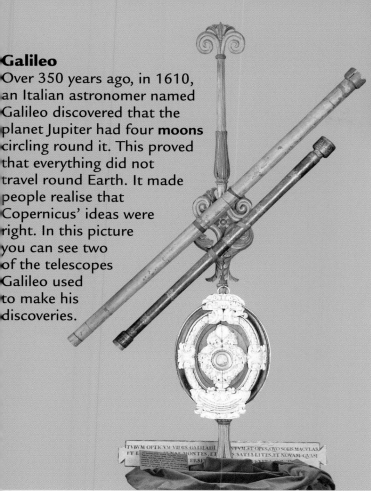

Newton

The English scientist, Isaac Newton, was born about 350 years ago in 1642. According to a story, he watched an apple drop from a tree and wondered why it fell straight to the ground. Then he realised that Earth was pulling everything towards it. He called this **gravity**. Newton also worked out why the planets travelled round the Sun and did not shoot off in all directions into space. He realised that the Sun's gravity pulled the planets and kept them in their paths round the Sun.

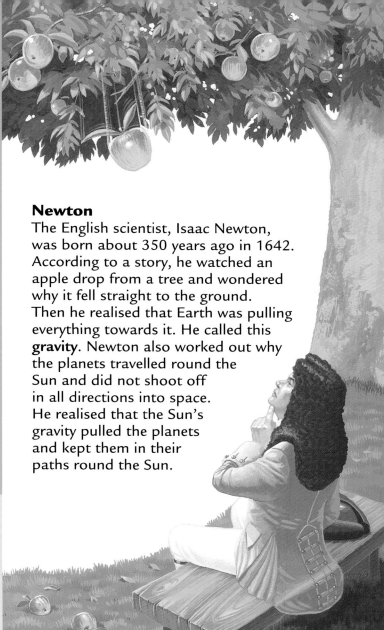

Modern astronomers

Today, many astronomers work in a control room with computers, such as the one below. They point a telescope at the sky and use it to make pictures of distant stars and galaxies. Computers then add colours to the pictures to make them clearer.

Adding colour

A computer has added colours to this picture of a galaxy. The brightest parts are coloured white.

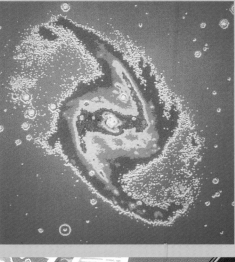

Go to Astronomer page 8, Galaxy page 42, Space shuttle page 20

Telescope

A telescope is a tool that astronomers use to find out about space. It makes distant things, such as stars and **planets**, look bigger and nearer. Over 350 years ago, an Italian astronomer named Galileo became the first person to study the night sky with a telescope. Today, telescopes are more powerful than Galileo's and astronomers can see much further into space.

tube
Light from stars and planets enters the telescope tube.

eyepiece
An astronomer looks through the eyepiece.

Simple telescope
People who study the stars at home often look through a simple telescope, such as the one on the left. Sometimes a camera is fitted to the telescope. It can take photographs which show more detail than the eye can see.

Stand
A stand keeps the telescope steady.

light

eyepiece

mirror

How a telescope works
A curved mirror inside the tube collects light from stars and planets and makes a picture, or image, of part of the sky. An eyepiece makes this image look bigger.

Observatory
Large modern telescopes are often built on mountain tops where the sky is clear. Several telescopes are usually grouped together at a place called an observatory. Each telescope is inside a dome-shaped building. A slit in the dome opens to let the telescope point at the sky and take photographs, which an astronomer can study. The dome turns round so that the telescope can point at any part of the sky.

Radio telescope

Many objects in space, such as distant galaxies, give out **radio waves**. Astronomers collect these waves with radio telescopes, which look like large dishes. A group of telescopes works together, using the radio waves to make a picture of the object in space. The radio telescopes in this photograph are part of the Very Large Array Telescope in the United States, which has 27 dishes linked together.

Hubble Space Telescope

There is a telescope in space which circles round Earth. It is named after the astronomer Edwin Hubble and it was **launched** in 1990 by the space shuttle. Hubble can see further than larger telescopes on Earth. This is because in space there are no clouds or moving air to blur its view. Hubble has taken photographs of many stars and galaxies.

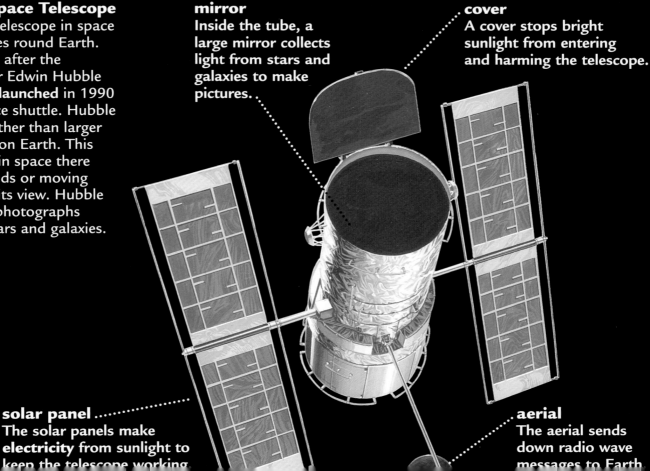

mirror
Inside the tube, a large mirror collects light from stars and galaxies to make pictures.

cover
A cover stops bright sunlight from entering and harming the telescope.

solar panel
The solar panels make **electricity** from sunlight to keep the telescope working.

aerial
The aerial sends down radio wave messages to Earth.

Go to Astronaut page 16, Rocket page 14, Solar system page 28, Sun page 26

Moon

The Moon is a ball of rock that circles round Earth once in about every 27 days. The same side of the Moon, called the nearside, always faces Earth. The other side, called the farside, is hidden from Earth. The Moon is the only place in space that astronauts have visited. Twelve astronauts have landed there to explore its surface and bring back rocks. They discovered that the Moon was dry and dusty, and that nothing lived there.

surface
The Moon's surface is covered with thousands of **craters**. They were made millions of years ago, when rocks from space crashed into the Moon.

crater
A crater has a ring of mountains round its edges. Sometimes there are also mountains in the middle of a crater.

mountain
Long lines of mountains run across some parts of the Moon. These mountains are called the Apennines.

Moon walking
This astronaut is collecting rock. He has to wear a spacesuit because on the Moon there is no air to breathe. His footprints will remain there for thousands of years because there is neither wind nor rain to blow them away.

streak
These streaks on the Moon's surface were made when melted rock was flung out of a newly formed crater.

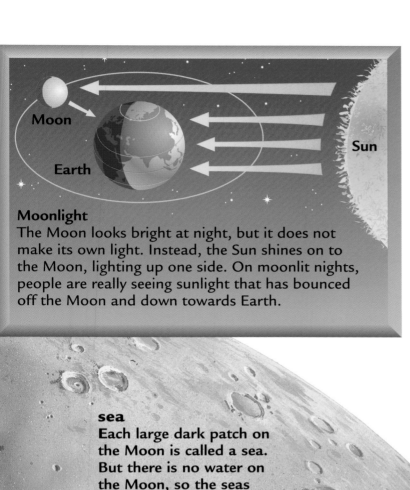

Moon

Earth

Sun

Moonlight
The Moon looks bright at night, but it does not make its own light. Instead, the Sun shines on to the Moon, lighting up one side. On moonlit nights, people are really seeing sunlight that has bounced off the Moon and down towards Earth.

Factfile

In the sunlight, the Moon is twice as hot as the hottest desert on Earth, but in the dark, it is almost twice as cold as the coldest place on Earth.

*In 1959, a Russian **spacecraft** called Luna 3 sent the first pictures of the farside of the Moon back to Earth.*

*The Moon is bigger than the smallest **planet**, which is Pluto.*

sea
Each large dark patch on the Moon is called a sea. But there is no water on the Moon, so the seas are dry.

full Moon

crescent Moon

Moon shapes
As the Moon travels round Earth, you can see different amounts of the side lit by the Sun. Sometimes, the Moon looks round. This is called a full Moon. At other times, it may have a crescent shape.

Tides
Twice a day on Earth, oceans rise up the shore and fall back down again. This is caused by the Moon's **gravity** pulling the oceans towards the Moon.

Go to Astronaut page 16, Moon page 12, Satellite page 22

Rocket

A rocket is a **vehicle** that can carry astronauts or satellites into space. It has powerful **engines** which burn **fuel**, pushing it upwards into the sky. Most rockets have two or three sections, called stages. Each stage has its own engines and fuel. The stages burn up their fuel one at a time and then drop away. This makes the rocket lighter, letting it travel faster and faster until it reaches space.

escape rocket
An escape rocket can carry the astronauts awa if something goes wrong

Apollo spacecraft
The astronauts travel to the Moon inside the Apollo **spacecraft**.

third stage
The third stage provides extra power to send the astronauts to the Moon.

Saturn V
Saturn V was one of the most powerful types of rockets ever built. Between 1968 and 1972, it was used for the Apollo missions to take astronauts to **orbit** and land on the Moon. Five main engines lifted the rocket off the **launch pad** until it was travelling 350 times faster than a car on a motorway.

second stage
The second stage is smaller than the first stage. It lifts the astronauts into space

first stage
Inside the first stage, there are two large tanks that hold the fuel for the five main engines.

engine
The five main engines are at the bottom of the rocket.

crawler
A person can walk faster than the huge crawler that carries the rocket to the launch pad.

14

To the Moon and back

During an Apollo mission, three astronauts travelled to the Moon in the small Apollo spacecraft, but only two of them landed. One astronaut stayed in the spacecraft, circling round the Moon, while the other two flew down to the surface in the **lunar lander**. The astronauts came back to Earth in the part of the spacecraft shown on the right. They landed in the sea and were picked up by a ship waiting nearby.

7 The satellite at the top of the third stage is carried higher. It is then released into orbit round Earth.

6 The second stage drops away, leaving only the third stage and the satellite.

5 The covers that protect the satellite are thrown off.

4 The second stage engines start firing to push the rest of the rocket upwards.

3 When the first stage has used up its fuel, it drops away as well.

2 The **booster rockets** soon use up their fuel and fall away into the sea.

1 The Ariane rocket blasts off, carrying its satellite into space.

Ariane

Ariane is a type of rocket that launches satellites. Astronauts do not travel on board. The rocket is controlled from Earth by scientists.

Astronaut

Astronauts are people who travel in space to explore new places, such as the Moon, or to carry out experiments. They also repair **machines**, such as telescopes and satellites. There is no air in space, so when astronauts leave their **spacecraft** they must wear spacesuits to let them breathe. Astronauts have to train for a long time before they are ready to travel into space.

Astronaut training

Floating in a water tank helps teach an astronaut how it feels to be **weightless**.

In space there is no right way up. A spinning chair helps astronauts to imagine how this feels.

Astronauts learn how to fly their spacecraft by studying the flight controls.

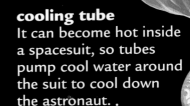

cooling tube
It can become hot inside a spacesuit, so tubes pump cool water around the suit to cool down the astronaut.

pocket
An astronaut has pockets on his spacesuit to hold small tools.

astronaut's glove
These gloves screw on to the spacesuit. They let the astronaut's fingers bend to do work.

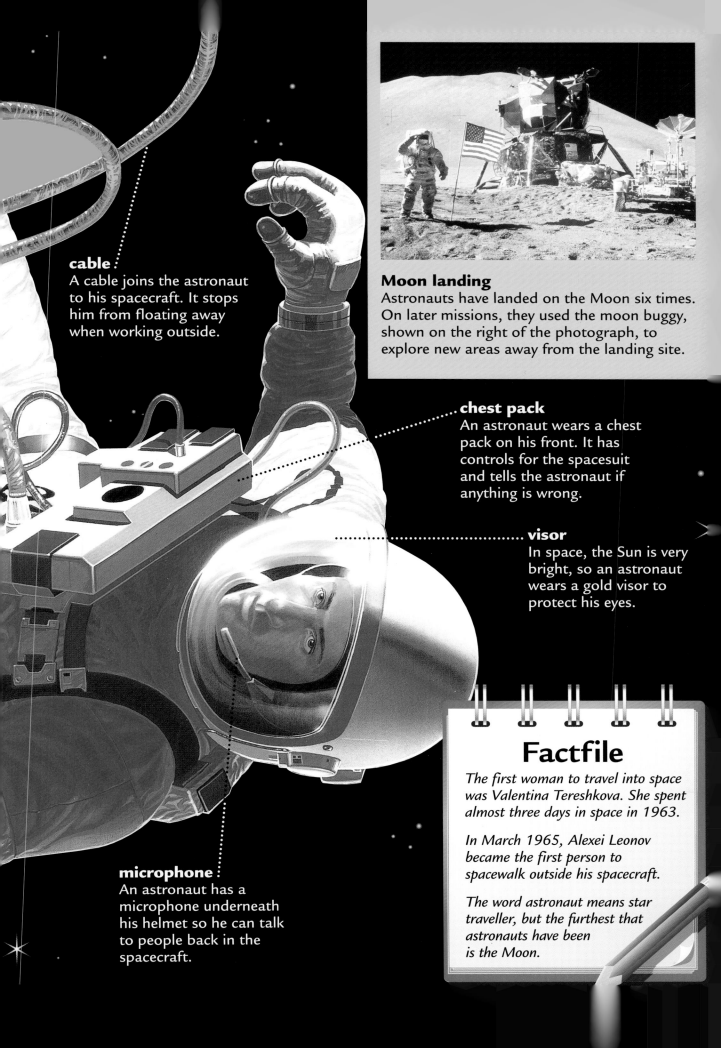

cable
A cable joins the astronaut to his spacecraft. It stops him from floating away when working outside.

Moon landing
Astronauts have landed on the Moon six times. On later missions, they used the moon buggy, shown on the right of the photograph, to explore new areas away from the landing site.

chest pack
An astronaut wears a chest pack on his front. It has controls for the spacesuit and tells the astronaut if anything is wrong.

visor
In space, the Sun is very bright, so an astronaut wears a gold visor to protect his eyes.

Factfile

The first woman to travel into space was Valentina Tereshkova. She spent almost three days in space in 1963.

In March 1965, Alexei Leonov became the first person to spacewalk outside his spacecraft.

The word astronaut means star traveller, but the furthest that astronauts have been is the Moon.

microphone
An astronaut has a microphone underneath his helmet so he can talk to people back in the spacecraft.

Space station

A space station is a home in space. Astronauts live here and carry out experiments to learn more about how space affects people. Inside the space station, there is air to breathe, so the astronauts do not need to wear spacesuits. In 1986, Russia **launched** a space station called Mir. Rockets brought up the different parts and joined them together in space.

▶ **Mir space station**

control desk
Astronauts control the space station from here.

solar panel
These panels use the Sun's rays to make **electricity**, which provides power for the space station.

living quarters
Astronauts sleep, eat and work in the living quarters. This was the first part to be launched into space.

Factfile

There have been nine space stations, including Mir, Skylab and seven models of Salyut.

In 1995, Valery Polyakov lived in space for 438 days, setting a record for the longest time spent in space.

There are plans to build a new space station, called Alpha, in the next ten years.

Astronauts stand in a big bag to take a shower. A tube sucks away the water when they have finished washing.

Astronauts must drink through straws to stop any liquids from floating away. They eat food that comes in closed foil packets.

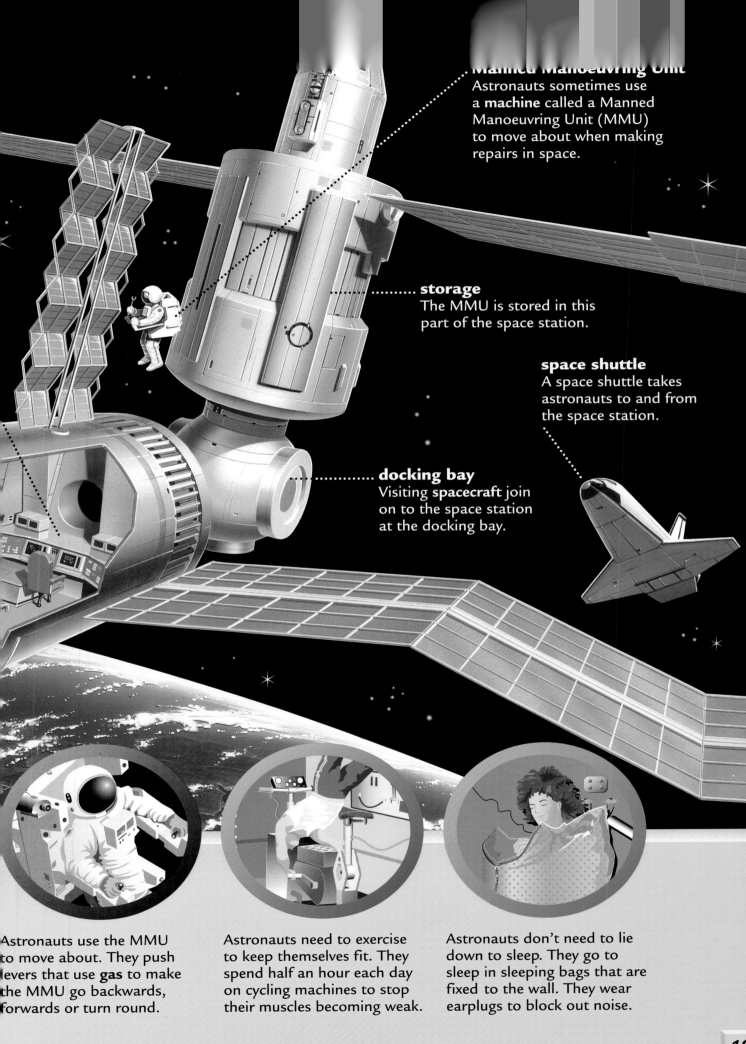

Manned Manoeuvring Unit
Astronauts sometimes use a **machine** called a Manned Manoeuvring Unit (MMU) to move about when making repairs in space.

storage
The MMU is stored in this part of the space station.

space shuttle
A space shuttle takes astronauts to and from the space station.

docking bay
Visiting **spacecraft** join on to the space station at the docking bay.

Astronauts use the MMU to move about. They push levers that use **gas** to make the MMU go backwards, forwards or turn round.

Astronauts need to exercise to keep themselves fit. They spend half an hour each day on cycling machines to stop their muscles becoming weak.

Astronauts don't need to lie down to sleep. They go to sleep in sleeping bags that are fixed to the wall. They wear earplugs to block out noise.

Go to Astronaut page 18, Satellite page 22, Space probe page 24, Space station page 18, Telescope page 10

Space shuttle

A space shuttle is a special plane that can fly into space and back to Earth many times. It can take astronauts to a space station or **launch** a satellite or space probe. A shuttle has several parts. The part that carries the astronauts is called the shuttle orbiter. The other parts are a huge **fuel** tank and two **booster rockets**. The fuel tank is the only part of the space shuttle that cannot be used again.

Take off and landing

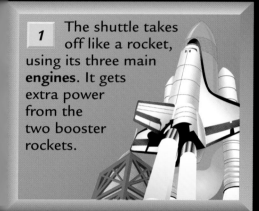

1 The shuttle takes off like a rocket, using its three main **engines**. It gets extra power from the two booster rockets.

2 When the fuel from the boosters is used up, they fall into the sea. The large fuel tank will fall away too.

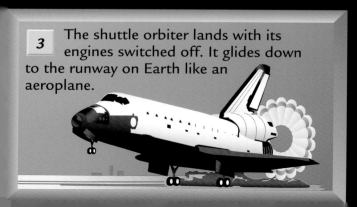

3 The shuttle orbiter lands with its engines switched off. It glides down to the runway on Earth like an aeroplane.

▼ **space shuttle orbiter**

payload bay
Cameras and telescopes in the payload, or cargo, bay take pictures of Earth or study the stars in space.

tile
When the shuttle comes back to Earth, it becomes very hot. Thousands of special tiles stop it from burning up.

engine
The three main engines are not used in space. Smaller engines move the shuttle and take it back towards Earth.

payload bay door
In space, the doors of the payload bay are open to let extra heat from the cabin escape.

Spacelab
Spacelab is a **laboratory** where the astronauts work. It fits inside the payload bay.

robot arm
The robot arm can launch or capture a satellite. Astronauts can attach themselves to the arm to make repairs to the satellite.

cabin
On the upper deck of the cabin, there are controls for flying the shuttle. The astronauts eat, sleep and work on a deck below.

tunnel
An astronaut floats through a tunnel to move from the shuttle cabin to Spacelab.

Factfile

There are four shuttle orbiters. They are called Columbia, Atlantis, Discovery and Endeavour.

On 28 January 1986, the shuttle Challenger exploded 73 seconds after take off, killing all seven astronauts on board.

During take off, the power of a shuttle's engines is the same as 140 jumbo jets.

Into space
In April 1990, the Hubble Space Telescope was launched by the space shuttle Discovery. An astronaut in the shuttle cabin worked the controls for the robot arm, which put the telescope into **orbit**.

Go to Rocket page 14, Space shuttle page 20

Satellite

A satellite is a **machine** that **orbits** Earth. There are many kinds of satellites and they do different jobs. Some study the weather or the Earth's surface, while others send messages from one part of the world to another. Satellites have different orbits depending on the job they do. Powerful rockets carry the satellites up into space and put them into the right orbit.

▶ These are four of the satellites orbiting Earth.

Navstar
A satellite, such as Navstar, helps ships and planes to find their way, or navigate.

Meteosat
Meteosat is a weather satellite. It watches the clouds and measures the strength of the wind. It also finds out the **temperature** of the land, sea and air.

A television forecaster uses the measurements from a weather satellite to tell people what the weather will be like over the next few days.

Messages sent by Navstar tell a captain where his ship is, even in bad weather. They can also tell him how fast the ship is travelling.

Satellite pictures from Landsat are studied by scientists. They can show how well crops are growing, spot forest fires and help to make maps of Earth.

22

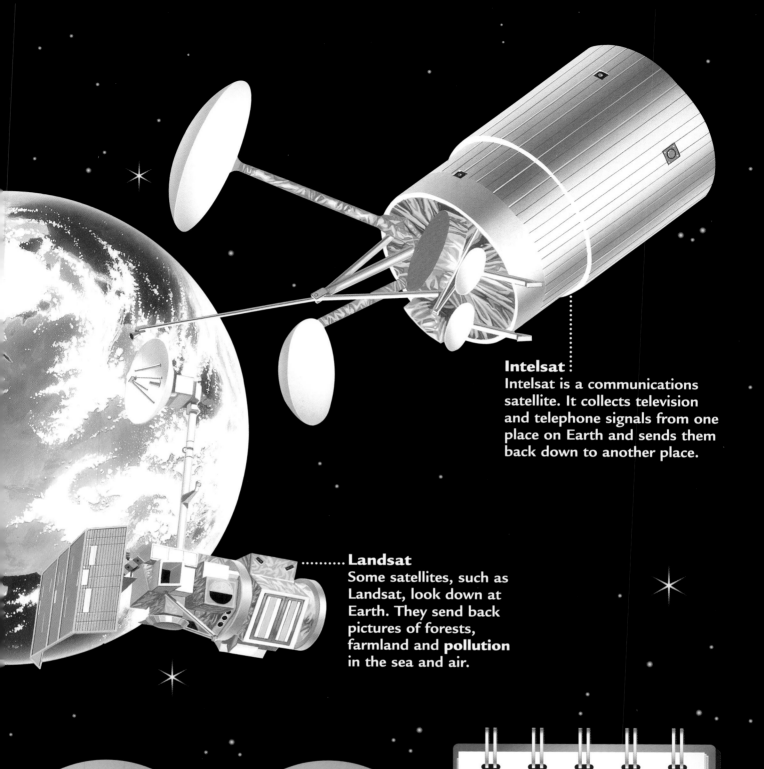

Intelsat
Intelsat is a communications satellite. It collects television and telephone signals from one place on Earth and sends them back down to another place.

Landsat
Some satellites, such as Landsat, look down at Earth. They send back pictures of forests, farmland and **pollution** in the sea and air.

A telephone conversation may travel up to a communications satellite and then down to someone on the end of a phone, in another country.

A communications satellite sends television programmes from one country to another, so people all over the world can watch them.

Factfile

In 1957, Russia launched Sputnik 1, which was the first ever satellite. It circled Earth in just over one and a half hours.

In 1990, there were about 2,000 working satellites orbiting Earth.

The first weather satellite to send pictures of clouds back to Earth was called Tiros. It was launched in April 1960.

Go to Comet and asteroid page 34, Gas planet page 32, Rocky planet page 30

Space probe

A space probe is a **machine** that explores space and sends back information and pictures to Earth. Astronauts do not travel in a space probe. Instead it is controlled by scientists on the ground. Some probes are **launched** by a rocket, others by a space shuttle. Probes have visited many **moons** and all the **planets** except for Pluto. They have sent back information about the weather, **temperature** and surface of these places.

Neptune

Uranus

Dark spot
In 1989, a space probe found a dark spot on the planet Neptune. It was a huge storm about the size of Earth, but it now seems to have disappeared.

Voyager 2 space probe

Saturn

Jupiter

Voyager
In 1977, two space probes called Voyager 1 and 2 set out to visit the giant planets furthest away from the Sun. Both probes flew past Jupiter and Saturn, and Voyager 2 also went on to visit Uranus and Neptune. Its journey from the Earth to Neptune took 12 years. The probes sent back close-up pictures of the planets' cloudy surfaces and discovered many new moons.

Viking

In 1976, two probes named Viking reached the planet Mars. The probes circled round Mars, making maps of its surface, while **landers** travelled to the ground. These tested rocks and soil to see if anything lived there, but they found nothing. You can see a Viking lander below. In 1996, more probes were sent to explore other parts of Mars.

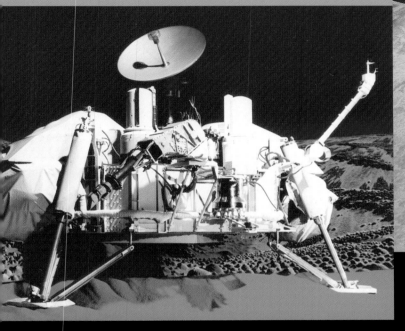

Magellan

The Magellan space probe arrived at Venus in 1990. It could not take photographs because thick clouds hid the planet's surface. Instead, it bounced **radio waves** off the planet. Computers back on Earth were then able to make pictures from these radio waves. This picture shows mountains and **volcanoes** on Venus' surface. The dark parts are the places that Magellan missed.

Galileo

The most recent probe to visit Jupiter is called Galileo. It arrived in 1995, after a six-year journey. The main probe dropped a smaller probe, shown on the right, by parachute into Jupiter's clouds. For nearly an hour it sent information about the clouds up to the main probe and then back to scientists waiting on Earth. The main probe then circled round Jupiter and visited its four large moons.

Jupiter

small probe

Ida

The Galileo space probe sent back the first ever close-up photographs of space rocks, or asteroids. It saw this one, called Ida, on its way to Jupiter.

Go to Earth page 6, Moon page 12, Solar system page 28, Star page 36

Sun

The Sun is a huge fiery ball of **gas** that glows in the sky. It is the closest star to Earth. Like all stars, the Sun gives out **energy** as heat and light. Much of this is lost in space but some of it reaches Earth. Without heat and light, Earth would be dark and cold and nothing could ever live here.

Warming Earth
The Sun always warms Earth, but it shines more strongly on some places than others. At the far north and south of Earth, the Sun shines weakly, so the land is always cold. At the middle of Earth, the Sun shines strongly. Here it is always warm.

Using sunlight
The panels on the roof of this house use sunlight to make **electricity** which powers **machines** such as the cooker and television.

flare
Sometimes hot gas bursts out of the Sun as a flare.

prominence
A prominence is a huge tongue or loop of gas that rises high above the Sun's surface.

WARNING!
Never look directly at the Sun. Its light is so bright that it could harm your eyes.

corona
The corona is the name of the layer of thin gas all round the Sun.

Sun's surface
Hot gas bubbles up on the Sun's surface and glows yellow.

core
The **core** is where the Sun makes its energy.

under the Sun's surface
Here, churning gas carries energy up to the surface of the Sun where it can escape.

Factfile

Light from the Sun travels almost 150 million km to reach Earth. It would take a car over 200 years to travel this far, while light reaches Earth in only eight minutes.

In ancient times, many Chinese people believed that an eclipse was a dragon eating the Sun.

The Sun spins round once every 27 days.

sunspot
Dark patches on the Sun are called sunspots. These areas are cooler than the rest of the Sun's surface.

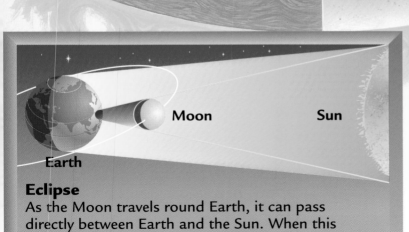

Eclipse
As the Moon travels round Earth, it can pass directly between Earth and the Sun. When this happens, the Sun is completely hidden for a few minutes. This is an eclipse of the Sun.

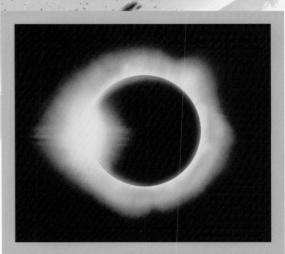

Ring of light
During an eclipse of the Sun, the Moon blocks out most of the Sun's light. Only the pale glow of the Sun's corona can be seen.

Solar system

The solar system is the name given to the Sun and all the objects in space that travel round it. In the solar system, there are nine **planets** and their **moons**, comets, and chunks of rock called asteroids and meteoroids. The planets lie huge distances apart and take different lengths of time to travel round the Sun. The time it takes for a planet to circle the Sun once is called its year. The planets also spin round like tops. The time taken for a planet to spin round once is its day.

▼ The planets are the largest objects in the solar system except for the Sun.

Jupiter
Jupiter is larger than all the other planets put together.

Mars
Mars is about half the size of Earth and much colder.

Moon

Earth
Earth is the third planet from the Sun. Many different plants and animals live here.

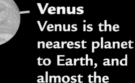

Sun

Venus
Venus is the nearest planet to Earth, and almost the same size.

Mercury
The only planet smaller than Mercury is Pluto.

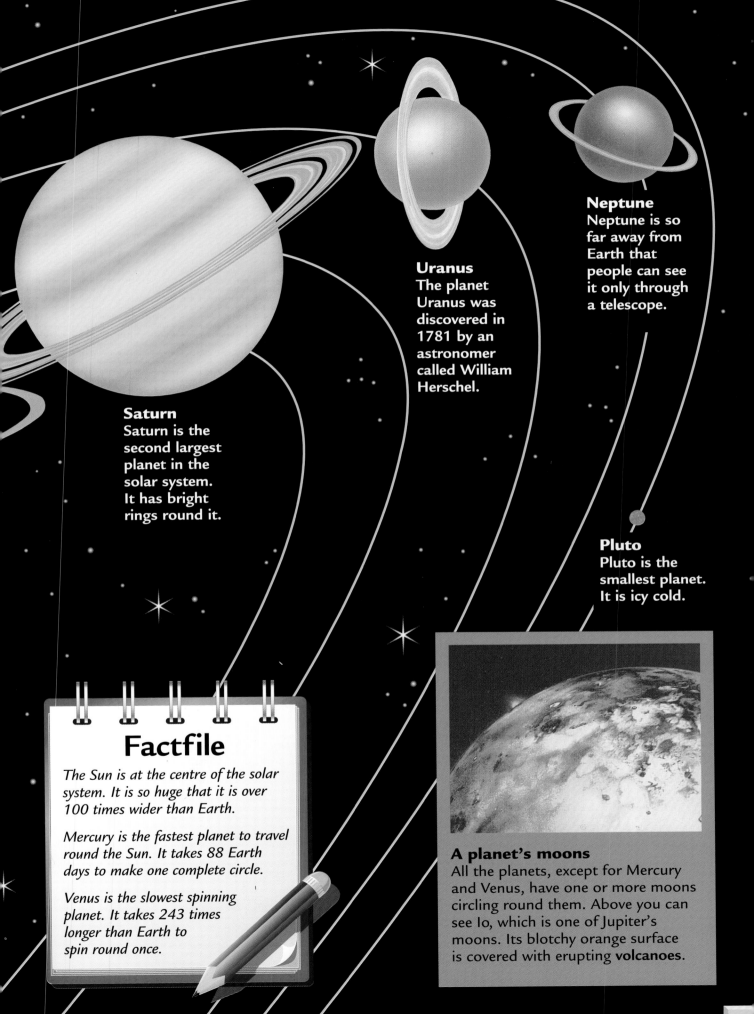

Neptune
Neptune is so far away from Earth that people can see it only through a telescope.

Uranus
The planet Uranus was discovered in 1781 by an astronomer called William Herschel.

Saturn
Saturn is the second largest planet in the solar system. It has bright rings round it.

Pluto
Pluto is the smallest planet. It is icy cold.

Factfile

The Sun is at the centre of the solar system. It is so huge that it is over 100 times wider than Earth.

Mercury is the fastest planet to travel round the Sun. It takes 88 Earth days to make one complete circle.

Venus is the slowest spinning planet. It takes 243 times longer than Earth to spin round once.

A planet's moons
All the planets, except for Mercury and Venus, have one or more moons circling round them. Above you can see Io, which is one of Jupiter's moons. Its blotchy orange surface is covered with erupting **volcanoes**.

29

Go to Earth page 6, Solar system page 28, Space probe page 24

Rocky planet

Some of the **planets** in the solar system have rocky surfaces and metal at their **core**. The four planets nearest to the Sun, which are Mercury, Venus, Earth and Mars, are all rocky planets. Pluto, the planet furthest away from the Sun, is similar to them, but its core is made of rock instead of metal. Pluto is so cold that its surface is covered in a thick layer of ice.

Crashing into Venus
This crater was made by a rock which hit Venus. All the rocky planets in the solar system have craters on their surface.

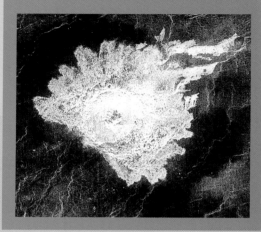

Venus
Venus is nearly the same size as Earth but it would not be a good planet for astronauts to visit because it is surrounded by thick, poisonous clouds. These keep Venus even hotter than Mercury, although it is further away from the Sun. The air on Venus presses down so hard that space probes have been crushed when they landed there.

crust
The outer layer, or crust, of Venus is made of rock.

Mercury
Mercury looks similar to the Moon. It is covered with thousands of **craters** that were made when rocks from space crashed into it millions of years ago. The side of Mercury that faces the Sun is over seven times hotter than the hottest desert on Earth. The side facing away from the Sun is extremely cold. There is no air or water on Mercury.

surface
Venus has mountains, craters and **volcanoes** on its surface.

core
The core of Venus is made of a metal called iron.

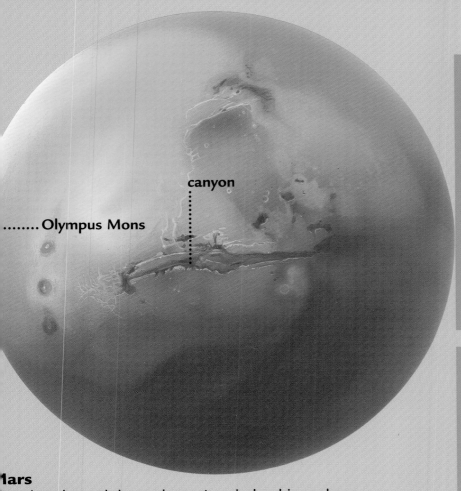

canyon

.... Olympus Mons

Mars

Mars is a dry and dusty planet. Its winds whip up huge dust storms that make its sky look pink. Large deserts, deep **canyons** and giant volcanoes cover Mars. The biggest volcano in the solar system is here. Its name is Olympus Mons. Mars is called the red planet because from Earth it looks red in the sky.

Two moons

Mars has two small rocky **moons**, that are shaped like potatoes and covered with craters. This is the larger moon called Phobos. The smaller moon is called Deimos.

On the surface

Rust-coloured sand and rocks lie on the surface of Mars.

Pluto

Pluto is a tiny planet right at the edge of the solar system. It is so small and far away that astronomers do not know much about it. Pluto was discovered in 1930. Then, in 1978, astronomers found that it had a moon which they named Charon. This is how Pluto and Charon might look from a visiting **spacecraft**.

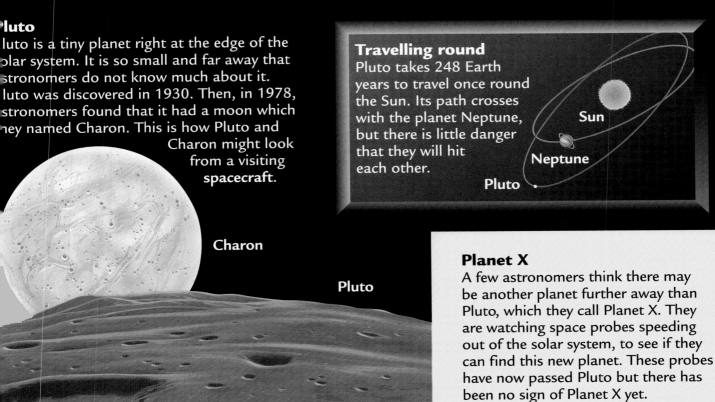

Charon

Pluto

Travelling round

Pluto takes 248 Earth years to travel once round the Sun. Its path crosses with the planet Neptune, but there is little danger that they will hit each other.

Sun

Neptune

Pluto

Planet X

A few astronomers think there may be another planet further away than Pluto, which they call Planet X. They are watching space probes speeding out of the solar system, to see if they can find this new planet. These probes have now passed Pluto but there has been no sign of Planet X yet.

Go to Astronomer page 8, Solar system page 28, Space probe page 24

Gas planet

A gas **planet** is made up mostly of **gases** and **liquids**. It has a rocky **core** which is covered in a thick layer of liquid or ice. On the outside of a gas planet, there are layers of coloured clouds. Jupiter, Saturn, Uranus and Neptune are gas planets. If astronauts ever manage to visit these distant places, they would not be able to explore them on foot, because there is no hard surface on which a **spacecraft** could land.

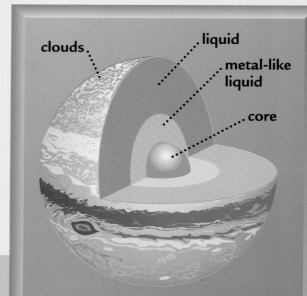

clouds · liquid · metal-like liquid · core

Inside Jupiter

Jupiter is made up of four different layers. At the centre, there is a small, rocky core. Then there are two layers of liquid. Jupiter's surface is made up of red and yellow swirling clouds.

Jupiter

Jupiter is the biggest planet in the solar system. Measuring across the middle, it is over 11 times larger than Earth. Jupiter spins faster than any other planet too. It is also very bright, which makes it easy to spot in the night sky. Venus is the only planet in the solar system which is brighter.

All the gas planets have rings round them. Jupiter's ring is so thin that it is difficult to see.

The red and white spots in Jupiter's clouds are storms. The largest of these storms is called the Great Red Spot. It is bigger than planet Earth and has lasted for at least 300 years.

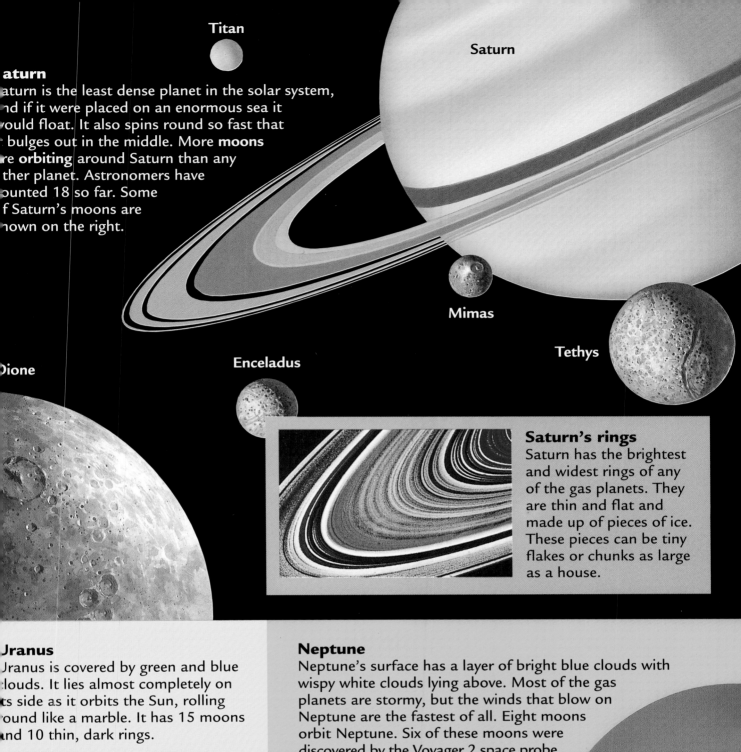

Titan

Saturn

Saturn
Saturn is the least dense planet in the solar system, and if it were placed on an enormous sea it would float. It also spins round so fast that it bulges out in the middle. More **moons** are **orbiting** around Saturn than any other planet. Astronomers have counted 18 so far. Some of Saturn's moons are shown on the right.

Mimas

Tethys

Dione

Enceladus

Saturn's rings
Saturn has the brightest and widest rings of any of the gas planets. They are thin and flat and made up of pieces of ice. These pieces can be tiny flakes or chunks as large as a house.

Uranus
Uranus is covered by green and blue clouds. It lies almost completely on its side as it orbits the Sun, rolling round like a marble. It has 15 moons and 10 thin, dark rings.

Neptune
Neptune's surface has a layer of bright blue clouds with wispy white clouds lying above. Most of the gas planets are stormy, but the winds that blow on Neptune are the fastest of all. Eight moons orbit Neptune. Six of these moons were discovered by the Voyager 2 space probe.

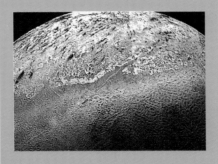

Triton
Triton is Neptune's largest moon and the coldest known place in the solar system.

Go to Earth page 6, Solar system page 28, Space probe page 24, Telescope page 10

Comet and asteroid

Comets and asteroids are part of the solar system. Like **planets** and **moons**, they travel round the Sun. Comets are made of dust and ice and look like dirty snowballs. Astronomers think there are millions of them travelling through space. Asteroids are chunks of rock. The biggest asteroids are hundreds of kilometres wide but most are as small as pebbles.

A comet's path

A comet travels from the edge of the solar system towards the Sun. It then swings round the Sun and heads away again.

A comet's tail

A comet is too small to see from Earth, except when it comes close to the Sun. Then the Sun's heat melts some of the comet's ice, making a huge cloud of dust and **gas**. This streams into a long tail, which is sometimes bright enough to see in the night sky. The tail of the comet points away from the Sun.

head

The icy centre of a comet is hidden inside its head, under a glowing dust cloud.

tail

A comet's tail can be millions of kilometres long

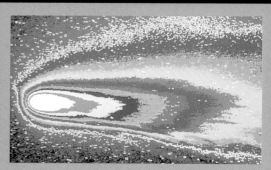

Halley's comet

Halley's comet comes close to the Sun once about every 76 years. This **false-colour** photograph was taken when it last appeared in 1986.

Meteor

As Earth travels through space, it bumps into small rocks and dust left behind from comets. When the rocks and dust hit the top of Earth's **atmosphere,** they burn up, making bright trails in the sky. Astronomers call these trails meteors, or shooting stars. Sometimes, the rocks are too large to burn up. They fall to the ground and are called meteorites.

In the sky
A meteor can look like a bright streak in the sky. It lasts for only a few seconds and then disappears.

Crashing to Earth
About 50 thousand years ago, a large meteorite crashed into a desert in America and made this **crater**.

Asteroid

Astronomers have counted several thousands of asteroids but think there are millions more. Most are too small to be seen from Earth, even with a telescope. The asteroid below is called Gaspra. Its photograph was taken by the Galileo space probe, as it flew past on its way to the planet Jupiter.

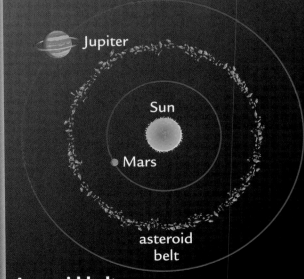

Jupiter

Sun

Mars

asteroid belt

Asteroid belt
Most asteroids lie in a ring, or belt, round the Sun between the planets Mars and Jupiter.

Go to Galaxy page 42, Sun page 26, Telescope page 10

Star

A star is a huge fiery ball of **gas** that gives out heat and light. The Sun is a star and the only one to look like a huge ball in the sky. All the other stars look like pinpoints of light because they are so far away. Stars are not all the same. They are different colours and sizes. Each star also has a lifetime. Once it is born, it will shine steadily for a long time, until it dies.

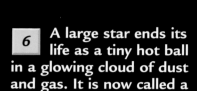

6 A large star ends its life as a tiny hot ball in a glowing cloud of dust and gas. It is now called a neutron star.

▶ During its life, a star changes several times. At each stage it looks different.

1 A star begins its life inside a large cloud of dust and gas called a nebula.

2 A clump of gas inside the nebula shrinks into a ball which becomes hotter and starts to glow. This ball is a new star.

Factfile

On a clear night you can see over 6,000 stars in the sky without using a telescope.

The hottest star that astronomers have found is nearly 40 times hotter than the Sun.

*In about five **billion** years, the Sun will swell up to a giant star. It may become large enough to swallow up Earth.*

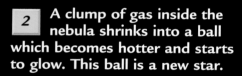

3 The star gives out light and heat steadily for thousands of millions of years, just like the Sun does now.

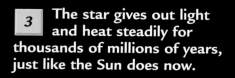

The stars in the sky look like single stars but many of them are really two stars. Pairs of stars often circle round one another. These kinds of stars are called binary, or double, stars.

A large group of stars is called a cluster. Most new stars, such as these shown in the picture, are in open clusters, while old stars are often tightly packed in round clusters.

5 A very large star may then explode, throwing out gas and dust in all directions. This explosion is called a supernova.

The Sun seems to be the largest star in the sky, but really it is a medium-sized star and is not particularly bright. The Sun only seems larger because it is closer to Earth than the other stars.

Some stars are hotter than others. The colour of a star shows how hot it is. The hottest stars are white and the coolest are red. In between are yellow stars such as the Sun.

When a large star dies, it may collapse, or fall in on itself, sucking in everything nearby. It even traps light. This is called a black hole. Nothing can escape from a black hole.

4 Towards the end of its life, a star swells up into a huge red ball known as a red giant.

Go to Constellations of the southern skies page 40, Star page 36

Constellations
of the northern skies

A constellation is a group of stars that makes a pattern in the sky. Astronomers have counted 88 constellations and given each of them a name. The constellations do not change their shape, but as the night passes, they seem to move across the sky. This happens because Earth is spinning round. The constellations themselves are not really moving. People see different constellations depending on where they live in the world.

▶ This picture shows the main constellations you can see in the northern half of the world. The United Kingdom is in this part of the world.

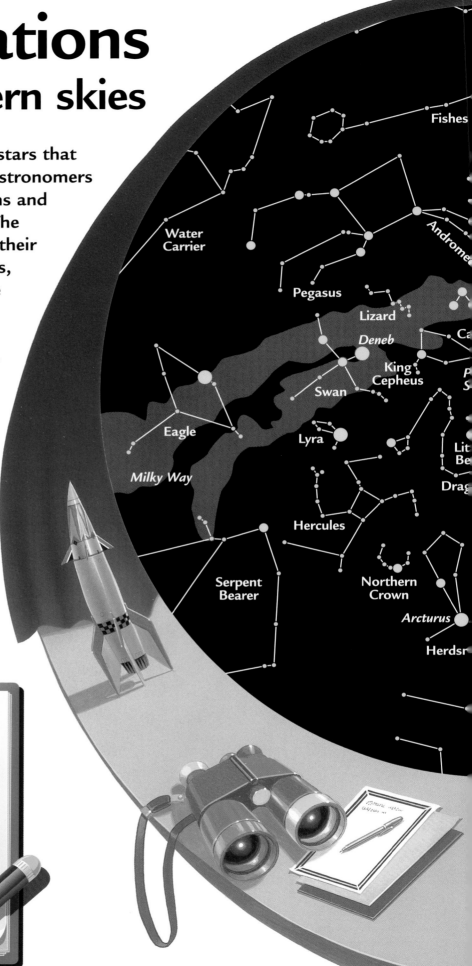

Fishes

Water Carrier

Andromeda

Pegasus

Lizard

Deneb

King Cepheus

Swan

Eagle

Lyra

Milky Way

Hercules

Dragon

Serpent Bearer

Northern Crown

Arcturus

Herdsman

Factfile

The brightest star you can see in the northern sky is called Betelgeuse. It is part of the Orion constellation.

The constellations seem to twinkle in the sky. This happens because moving air blurs starlight as it travels to Earth.

The faint Lynx constellation took its name from an animal with sharp eyesight, because you need sharp eyesight to spot it.

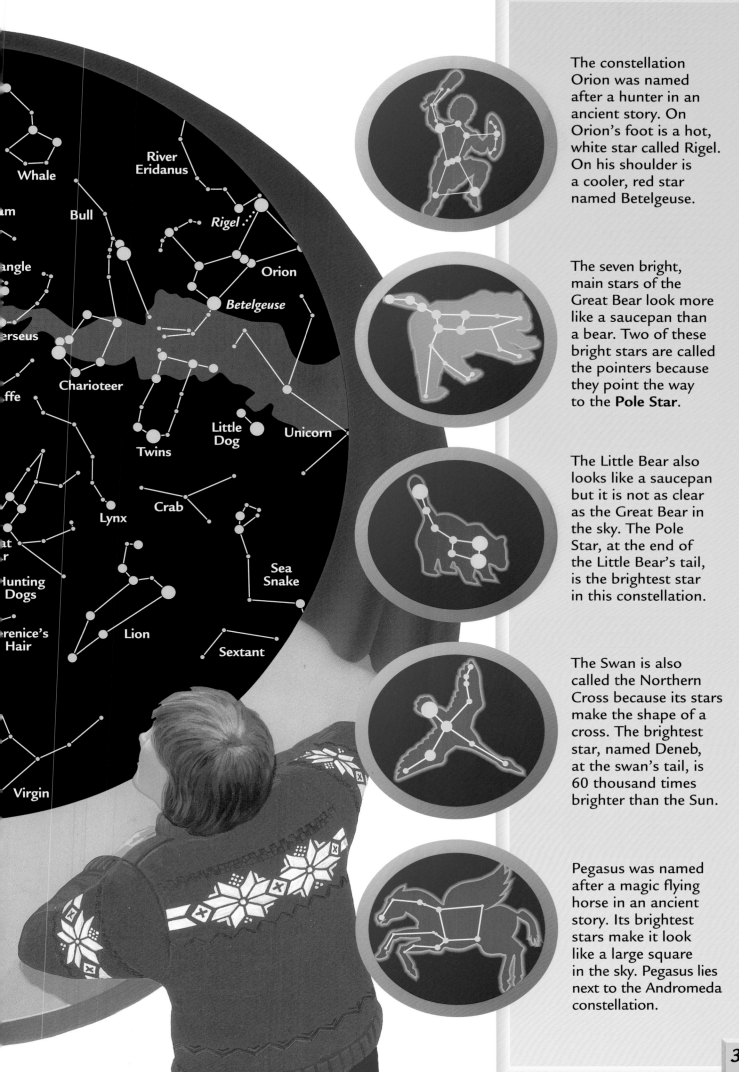

Whale

River
Eridanus

Bull

Rigel

Orion

Betelgeuse

Charioteer

Little
Dog

Unicorn

Twins

Crab

Lynx

Sea
Snake

Lion

Sextant

Hunting
Dogs

renice's
Hair

Virgin

The constellation Orion was named after a hunter in an ancient story. On Orion's foot is a hot, white star called Rigel. On his shoulder is a cooler, red star named Betelgeuse.

The seven bright, main stars of the Great Bear look more like a saucepan than a bear. Two of these bright stars are called the pointers because they point the way to the **Pole Star**.

The Little Bear also looks like a saucepan but it is not as clear as the Great Bear in the sky. The Pole Star, at the end of the Little Bear's tail, is the brightest star in this constellation.

The Swan is also called the Northern Cross because its stars make the shape of a cross. The brightest star, named Deneb, at the swan's tail, is 60 thousand times brighter than the Sun.

Pegasus was named after a magic flying horse in an ancient story. Its brightest stars make it look like a large square in the sky. Pegasus lies next to the Andromeda constellation.

Go to Constellations of the northern skies page 38, Star page 36

Constellations
of the southern skies

Many constellations, or groups of stars, were named thousands of years ago. Some, such as the Great Dog or the Whale, were named after an animal. Others, such as the Centaur, took their names from creatures or people in ancient stories. In the past, sailors travelling across the ocean used the constellations to find their way. During these long voyages, some new constellations were discovered. They were given names, such as the Sails, after parts of a ship.

▶ This picture shows the main constellations you can see in the southern half of the world. Places, such as Australia and most of South America, are in this part of the world.

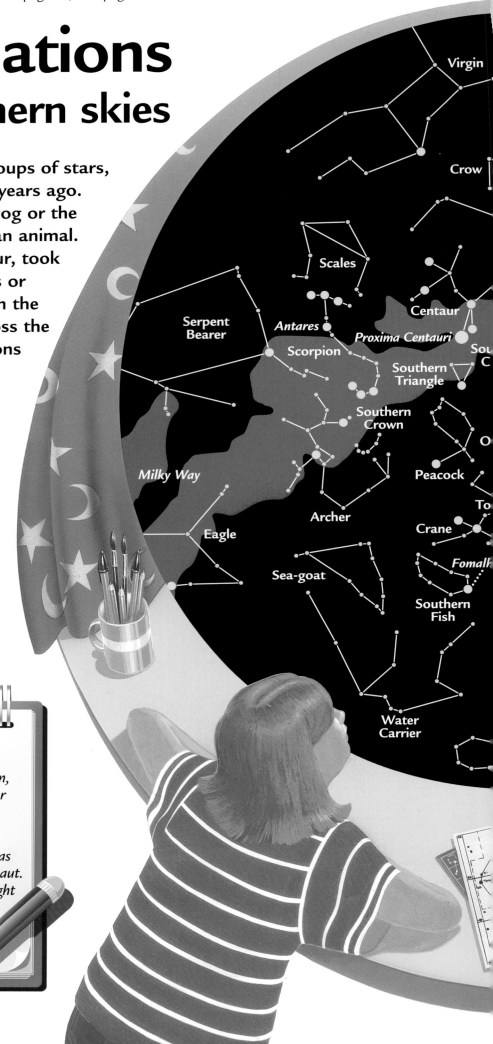

Factfile

Some constellations, such as Orion, can be seen in the southern sky for half of the year and the northern sky for the other half.

The Southern Fish constellation has just one bright star, called Fomalhaut. Long ago, an ancient people thought that Fomalhaut guarded heaven.

The Sea Snake is the largest constellation in the sky.

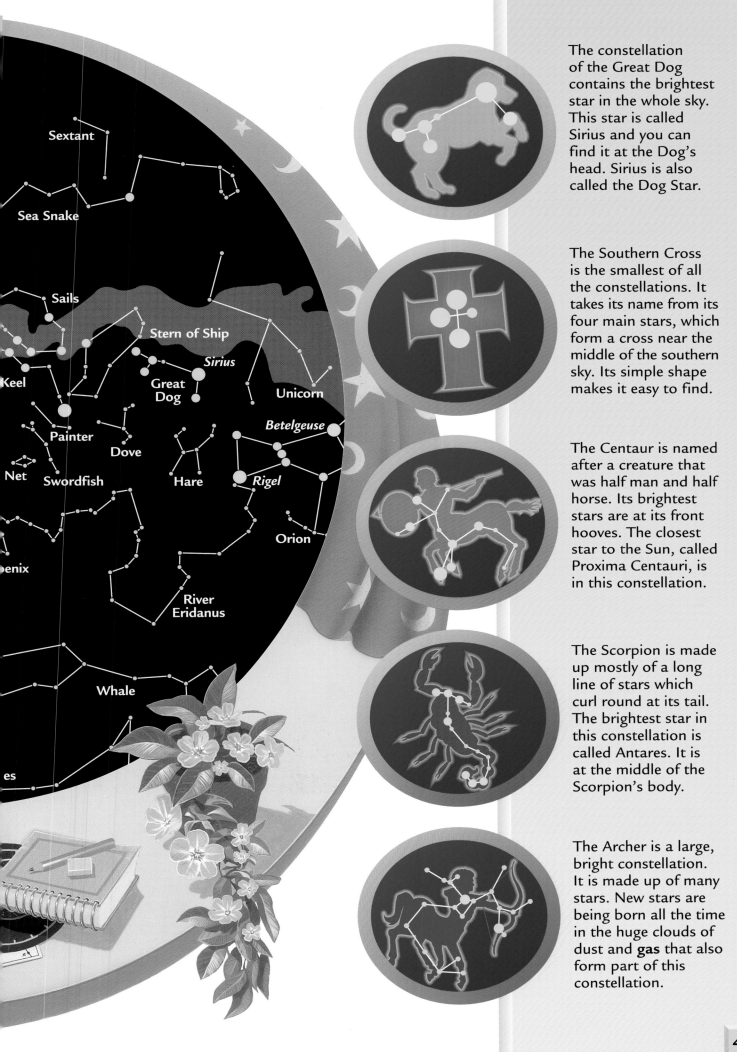

Sextant

Sea Snake

Sails

Stern of Ship

Sirius

Great Dog

Keel

Unicorn

Painter

Dove

Betelgeuse

Net

Swordfish

Hare

Rigel

enix

Orion

River Eridanus

Whale

es

The constellation of the Great Dog contains the brightest star in the whole sky. This star is called Sirius and you can find it at the Dog's head. Sirius is also called the Dog Star.

The Southern Cross is the smallest of all the constellations. It takes its name from its four main stars, which form a cross near the middle of the southern sky. Its simple shape makes it easy to find.

The Centaur is named after a creature that was half man and half horse. Its brightest stars are at its front hooves. The closest star to the Sun, called Proxima Centauri, is in this constellation.

The Scorpion is made up mostly of a long line of stars which curl round at its tail. The brightest star in this constellation is called Antares. It is at the middle of the Scorpion's body.

The Archer is a large, bright constellation. It is made up of many stars. New stars are being born all the time in the huge clouds of dust and **gas** that also form part of this constellation.

Go to Astronomer page 8, Star page 36, Telescope page 10

Galaxy

A galaxy is a huge group of stars, dust and **gas** that is held together by **gravity**. The biggest galaxies contain **billions** of stars. Astronomers have counted millions of galaxies in the **universe** using powerful telescopes, but they think there are still many more to be found. Some galaxies shoot out jets of hot gas from their centres, which travel far into space at high speeds.

Nebula

A cloud of gas and dust inside a galaxy is called a nebula. Some nebulae shine brightly, but others are dark. The Horsehead Nebula, above, is a dark cloud shaped like a horse's head. You can see it only because it shows up against the glowing red clouds behind it.

Milky Way

The Sun and Earth lie inside a galaxy called the Milky Way. It is shaped like a spiral, with a bulge in the middle and long, curved arms containing millions of stars. All these stars are moving round the centre of the galaxy. You can see part of the Milky Way from Earth. It looks like a faint band of light across the sky.

spiral arm
The spiral arms contain glowing gas clouds where new stars are born.

Sun and Earth
The Sun and Earth lie in one of the spiral arms near the edge of the Milky Way.

Types of galaxies

Galaxies have different shapes. A spiral galaxy has arms curling out from a ball at its centre. Some also have a bar across the middle and are called barred spirals. An elliptical galaxy has a round or squashed oval shape. Galaxies without any proper shape are called irregular.

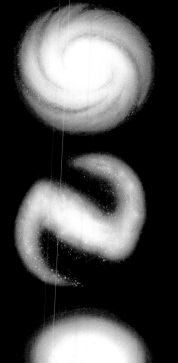

spiral galaxy

barred spiral galaxy

elliptical galaxy

Other galaxies

The billions of galaxies in the universe are not spread evenly through space. They lie together in groups called clusters. Sometimes, a large galaxy in the centre of one cluster has swallowed up nearby smaller galaxies. The Andromeda Galaxy in this picture is one of the nearest galaxies to the Milky Way and belongs to the same group. It is also about the same size and shape as the Milky Way. The two bright patches are small elliptical galaxies close to the Andromeda Galaxy.

Expanding universe

Astronomers have discovered that distant galaxies are moving away from the Milky Way and also from each other. This proves that the whole universe is expanding, or becoming bigger. In billions of years, the universe may stop expanding or it may carry on for ever. If it does stop, the universe might squash together and end in a Big Crunch.

further apart
Here the universe has expanded, so the galaxies are further apart from each other.

Amazing facts

On these pages, you can discover amazing facts about space. You can find out how hot the **planets** are, how big they are and how fast they are travelling. You can also learn about the people and animals that have been into space.

Space records

Largest crew
When the space shuttle Atlantis linked up with the Mir space station in June 1995, there were 10 people on board. Six were Americans and four were Russians.

How fast are you moving?

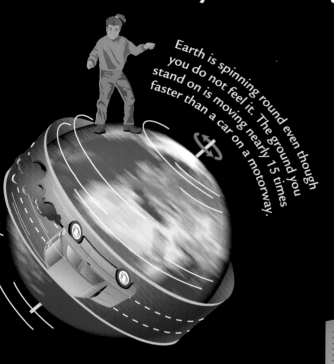

Earth is spinning round even though you do not feel it. The ground you stand on is moving nearly 15 times faster than a car on a motorway.

At the same time as Earth spins it also races round the Sun. It travels over 100 times faster than a jumbo jet even though you always seem to be still.

Which planet is...

the hottest?
On Venus, the **temperature** reaches over 460°C which is about eight times hotter than the hottest temperature ever recorded on Earth.

the coldest?
Pluto receives little heat from the Sun. Its temperature sinks to -220°C, which is more than twice as cold as the coldest place on Earth.

Exploring space

Here are some of the most important dates in the history of space travel.

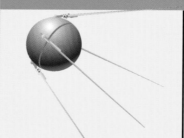

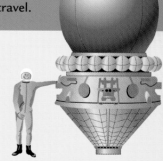

1957

The first satellite, Sputnik 1, is **launched** by the Russians. This begins the space age.

1961

Yuri Gagarin becomes the firs[t] person to fly in space. He cir[cles] once round Earth in less than two hours.

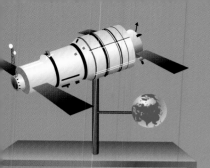

First space station

Salyut 1 was a Russian space station launched in 1971. A crew of three people lived and worked in it for three weeks while it circled round Earth.

Longest stay on the Moon

In 1972, on the last Apollo trip, Eugene Cernan and Harrison Schmitt spent three days on the Moon, exploring its surface in their buggy.

Which animals have travelled into space?

Dog

In 1957, a dog called Laika became the first living thing to travel into space. Laika proved that it was safe for people to travel into space too.

Spider

In 1973, two spiders, called Anita and Arabella, lived in the Skylab space station. They showed that spiders could spin webs in space as well as on Earth.

Jellyfish

In 1991, over 2,000 jellyfish were taken on board the space shuttle to see how well they could swim in space. Scientists discovered that the fish became confused and swam in circles instead of straight ahead.

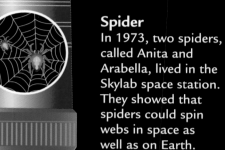

Different sizes

It is difficult to imagine the sizes of objects in space because they are so enormous. This picture compares the sizes of the Sun, Moon, Earth and Jupiter. Imagine the Sun is a large beachball...

...then Jupiter is the size of a tennis ball...

...Earth is the size of a pea...

...and the Moon is the size of a pinhead.

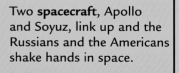

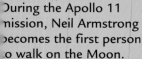

1969

During the Apollo 11 mission, Neil Armstrong becomes the first person to walk on the Moon.

1975

Two **spacecraft**, Apollo and Soyuz, link up and the Russians and the Americans shake hands in space.

1981

The space shuttle Columbia makes its first ever flight. It stays in space for over two days.

1995

The space shuttle Atlantis links up with the Mir space station for the first time.

Glossary

atmosphere A layer of gas that surrounds a planet, star or moon. Earth's atmosphere, called the air, is a mixture of different gases.

billion A number equal to one thousand million, written as 1,000,000,000.

booster rocket A small rocket that is attached to a large space rocket to give extra power at liftoff.

canyon A deep rocky passage with steep sides that lies in between mountains or hills.

core The centre of a planet, star or moon.

crater A round hole in the ground that is made when a rock from space hits a planet or moon.

electricity A type of energy used to make things such as light and heat, or to make machines work.

elliptical A curved shape, like a squashed oval.

energy A power that makes things move or work. Some types of energy can be seen as light, or felt as heat.

engine The part of a machine, such as a rocket, that burns fuel to make it work or move.

false colour Colour added to a photograph of an object, such as a galaxy, to make it look clearer.

fuel A substance that can be burned to make heat or power.

gas A substance, such as air, that is not solid or liquid. Many gases are invisible and can only be felt if they move.

gravity The force that pulls things towards Earth's surface or towards each other.

laboratory A building or room where scientists work, using special equipment.

lander The part of a spacecraft that lands on the surface of a planet or moon.

launch To leave Earth on a journey into space.

launch pad The place where rockets take off.

liquid A substance that is runny and has no fixed shape, such as water.

lunar lander The part of the Apollo spacecraft that landed on the Moon.

machine Something with moving parts that does useful work, such as a spacecraft that travels to another planet or the Moon.

moon A natural object in space that travels round a planet. A moon is smaller than its planet.

orbit The curved path of an object as it travels in space round a larger object. The planets orbit the Sun, while satellites orbit Earth.

oxygen A gas in the air that most living things need to breathe to stay alive.

planet A large round object in space, such as Earth, that travels round the Sun or another star.

Pole Star The name of the star that lies almost directly above the North Pole, which is the most northern place on Earth.

pollution Unwanted material that spills into the air, sea or land and damages it.

radio wave An invisible ray that travels through air or space, carrying information that can be made into sounds or pictures.

solid A material that has a firm shape you can feel.

spacecraft Any vehicle, such as a rocket or space probe, that flies into space.

temperature A measure of how hot or cold something is.

universe The whole of space and everything in space including the Sun, Earth, stars and galaxies.

vehicle A machine, such as a rocket, that moves people or things from place to place.

volcano An opening on the surface of a planet or moon from which ash or hot rock erupts.

weightless Free falling, or floating in space and feeling as if you weigh nothing.

Index

Published by Two-Can Publishing
a division of Zenith Entertainment plc
43-45 Dorset Street
London W1H 4AB

Created by **act-two**
346 Old Street
London EC1V 9RB

Disk
Creative Director: William Wharfe
Art Director: Sarah Evans
Project Editor: Lyndall Thomas
Senior Designer: James Evans
Illustrators: Michele Egar, James Evans,
Richard Harris, James Jarvis
Programmers: Roger Emery, Paul Steven,
Martin Sinclair, Kirsten Minshall
Consultant: Kevin Johnson, Associate
Curator of Astronomy and Mathematics,
Science Museum, London
Production Director: Lorraine Estelle
Production Manager: Katherine Harvey

Book
Art director: Belinda Webster
Managing editor: Deborah Kespert
Senior Designer: Helen Holmes
Designer: Michele Egar
Editorial Support: Samantha Hilton,
Julia Hillyard
Consultant: Doug Millard,
Associate Curator of Space Technology,
Science Museum, London
Main Illustrations: Gary Bines
Computer illustrations: Mel Pickering

'Two-Can' and 'Interfact' are trademarks
of Two-Can Publishing.

ISBN 1-85434-639-3

Dewey Decimal Classification 523.1

A catalogue record for this book is
available from the British Library

Hardback 4 6 8 10 9 7 5 3

Printed in Hong Kong

Photographic Credits:
Ancient Art & Architecture Collection: p9 tl;
Genesis: p15 l;
Jet Propulsion Laboratory: p24 tr,
p25 tr & bl, p29 br, p30 cl & tr,
p33 cr & bc;
NASA: p12 bl, p25 tl, p35 bl;
Rex Features: p17 tr;
Robert Harding: p15 tr;
SPL: p9 br, p10 br, p21 br, p27 br,
p31 cr & tr, p34 br, p35 cr & tr, p42 tr;
Tony Stone Images: p11 t, p26 bl;
Zefa: p8 cl

Troubleshooting tips

System requirements

The Space disk will work on most Windows or Apple Macintosh computers. To check that it will run on yours, please read the minimum specifications below.

Windows
133Mhz Pentium processor with Windows version 3.1, 3.11, 95, 98; Soundblaster-compatible soundcard; 32Mb RAM.

Macintosh
100Mhz PowerPC, system 7.6.1 (or later); 32Mb RAM

Quick fixes

To get the most out of your Space disk, please check:
1. Your monitor is set to 640 x 480 and 256 colours.
2. You have the Arial font (Windows users) installed in your fonts folder.
3. You have no other applications open.

Read me file

If you have a problem with your Space disk, be sure to check the Read me file. To open this, click on the Read me icon which you will find next to the Space icon. If you are using Windows 95 or 98, you will need to open the Read me file using Windows Explorer.

Helpline

You can call the helpline on 0171 224 2441. The lines are open from 10.00 am to 5.00 pm, Monday to Friday, and calls are charged at normal rates. Remember to get permission from the person who pays the bill before you use the phone.

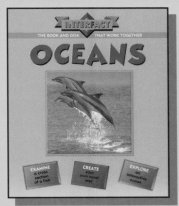
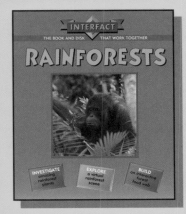
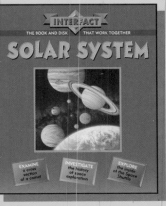
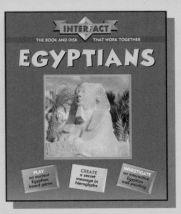
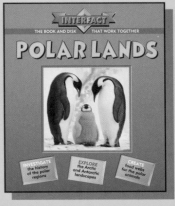
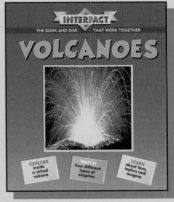

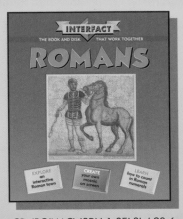

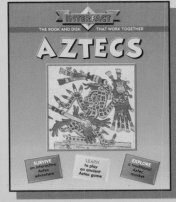

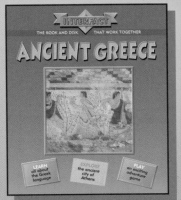